1.00

Chan Mi Gong
Chinese Meditation for Health

Liu Han Wen

Victory Press

Monterey, CA

ISBN 0-9620765-6-2

Contents

Preface

Chan Mi Gong is one of several types of traditional Buddhist qigong. By practicing qigong, one does not use medicine, nor does one rely on theory to cure illness; instead one uses one's own consciousness to control and regulate the body. Traditional Buddhism emphasizes developing ones inherent character and inner consciousness. It also stresses looking within and examining the self.

Hundreds of years of experience has shown that Chan Mi Gong can develop internal qi, regulate body metabolism, promote health, prevent illness, bring forth latent ability, and develop intelligence. Recently scientific experiments have given concrete supporting evidence.

Liu Han Wen based this book on information passed down in the family from generation to generation. He systematized the qigong and simplified the language. The qigong taught here is divided into six different sets:

1) Basics - basic techniques for developing qi, strengthening the body, and preventing illness

2) Wisdom techniques - used to awaken the intelligence and develop latent abilities

3) Combining Yin and Yang - grounds the body with the earth and connects it with the heavens

4) Double Cloud techniques - develops external qi to cure internal illness

5) Tu Na techniques - develops qi to be used for various purposes

6) Washing the Mind - powerful medical technique, can be used to cure other people's illness

Today, as we develop neuroscience, research the scientific basis of qigong and study extra sensory perception, traditional Chinese Chan Mi Gong can be considered a bridge between ancient and modern science. Therefore, this book includes Buddhist masters' treatises on the origin of the Chan (Zen) sect and the Mi (Tantric) sect of Buddhism, physiologist explanation of the effect of qigong on the body's functions, scientific research on qi and ESP, actual medical records of the effects of qigong, and many personal stories of how Chan Mi gong cured individual patients.

Hopefully, all this will give qigong a concrete base from which to develop and expand.

Translator's   Preface

Zhong Guo Chan Mi Gong by Liu Han Wen was published on July 1, 1988 by Heilong Jiang People's Publishing House, People's Republic of China. This 330,000 character 600 page book was the final result of several previous editions.

This translation covers only part of the book. It omits three sets of qigong, greatly simplifies the historical background and scientific research. The goal is to give an English introduction to this fascinating subject.

Oct. 1989

Author's   Preface

My great-grandfather Liu Jincai was born in Gaomi, Shandong Province. He first studied medicine, then became a monk. My grandfather Liu Zhaojue went from the city of Jinan to Mount Penglai. My father Liu Shanqing moved to Liaoning Province. He practiced both medicine and meditation. My aunt Liu Suluan became a nun at a young age. She practiced Taoism and medicine.

My ancestors practiced different types of qigong and medicine. These they taught me at home. They have been systematized under the name Chan Mi Gong, a combination of the theory and practice of the Chan and Mi sects of Buddhism.

In the 1950's at the Shenyang Sports Clinic (Liaoning Province) and in the 1960's at the Dandong Sports Clinic, I taught this type of qigong. The Cultural Revolution (1966-76) interrupted progress.

In 1980, Li Zhinan organized a qigong organization in Beijing and the Double Cloud technique was taught. Since then Chan Mi Gong has spread throughout the country. Articles have been written in various qigong and sports magazines. By the end of 1986, almost 1 million people had been introduced to this type of qigong. In 1987, Hong Kong publishers mentioned Chan Mi Gong in their books *Tu Jie Zhong Guo Liuxing Qigong* and *Zhong Guo Liuxing Qigong Xuan*.

Because of this interest, a committee was set up within the Chinese Qigong Research Association to write this book.

I would like to thank the following people for their help: the pioneer Li Zhinan, a courageous leader Professor Yuan Hongshou, my tireless colleague Ma Huiwen, my friends from Shandong and Liaoning, the editors and printers who have helped with previous editions, the helpful members of the Chinese Qigong Research Association, the Central Station for Teaching Chinese Chan Mi Gong, all the 240 plus satellite teachings stations, and the numerous research groups. And one last thanks to Comrade Qiu Yang.

Liu Hanwen
Oct. 10, 1988
Beijing

Part I

Techniques
of
Chan Mi Gong

Chapter 1

Basic Techniques

Section 1 Relaxation Techniques

1. Posture

The basic techniques can be practiced, standing, sitting or lying down.

  a) The entire body should be relaxed.

  b) The eyes should be lightly closed.

  c) Breathing should be natural.

2. Expanding the Third Eye

Smile to expand the third eye. The third eye, the slight depression in the center of the forehead above the eyebrows, symbolizes wisdom, kindness and fortune. (Figure 1) This is the window where people can emit *xinxi*, a special type of energy that is not limited to light, electricity, or electromagnetic waves. (This was called spiritual light in the past.) Emitting is used to search the universe. This window can also absorb. Ab-

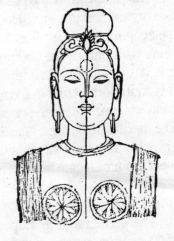

Figure 1

9

sorbing is used to differentiate and understand the universe.

The practice of emitting and absorbing qigong *xinxi* has useful applications. It can be used to regulate oneself or to help or cure others.

Important points

A worried or angry face will contract the forehead. When expanding the third eye, it is important to have a happy expression. But even more important is the inner smile that manifests an outer smile on the face. To put it another way, it is not just a physical smile at the third eye, but a smile from deep down in the heart, a smile that will last forever, a "nirvana smile".

A smile from the heart, a relaxed body, and normal breathing, help one to quickly enter a trance, which is important for gaining results of practice.

3. Relaxation of the Perineum

The perineum is the place between the reproductive organs and the anus. However, it is not limited to the acupuncture point Ren 1 (Huiyin) because it connects with part of the abdominal area. Like the third eye, it is capable of absorbing *xinxi* from the universe. It is an important link in the macrocosmic orbit which connects a person with pre-natal qi and post-natal qi. The perineum shares "the breath and fate" of the universe. It is the road on which man and heaven can meet, communicate and eventually combine.

Important point

The perineum is an important junction in moving qi. It is often compared to an iron door because it is so difficult to relax. "Trying to urinate, without urinating" is not enough, one must learn to use one's conscious mind, not physical effort to relax the perineum. If properly relaxed, the perineum and the inner sides of the legs should feel warm or numb.

When the third eye has expanded and the perineum is relaxed, then one should feel a sense of pleasure. The body should feel light and the heart should feel in harmony with the universe.

These two techniques are the most fundamental. They will be used throughout all six sets of Chan Mi Gong.

4. 70 - 30 Distribution of Weight

In order to properly prepare the body for practice and allow the flow of blood and qi, certain guidelines should be followed while in the standing position.

a) The stance is shoulder width with the feet turned outward very slightly. 70% of the weight of the body should be on the heals, 30% on the sole. The toes should be loose and free to move.

b) The knees are neither bent nor rigidly straight. They are supple and move slightly. (Figure 2)

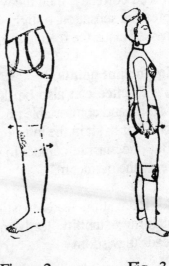

Figure 2   Fig. 3

c) Straighten the natural curve in the backbone near the waist by thrusting the hips slightly forward. (Figure 3)

d) Relax the shoulders by creating a little space under the arm pits and having the elbows face outward. The arms hang naturally and the fingers are slightly apart.

e) The neck is straight. Imagine the head is being pulled upward.

f) The head, perineum and point between the two heels should all be in a straight line. (Figure 4) The body should not lean forward or to the sides.

Fig. 4

If all the directions up to this point have been followed correctly, then the whole body should have a pleasant sensation, a slight warmth or a gentle numbness. This is the feeling of qi moving in the body.

Important points

Practice can also be done sitting or lying in a natural and comfortable position. There is no need to kneel or to sit in the lotus (crossed legged) positions. But one must remember to expand the third eye and relax the perineum.

Relaxation leads to stillness; stillness leads to stability; stability leads to realization; realization leads to wisdom.

12

Section 2 Moving Techniques

These four exercises designed to moved the backbone, promote the flow of qi, exercise internal organs
of the body and help regulate metabolism. They also
promote positive emotions and an overall feeling of
well being.

1. Front to Back Rocking Motion

With eyes still closed, look inward. Bring the attention to the coccyx (tip of the tailbone). Slowly and
gently rock the coccyx backward and forward in a
wavelike motion. (Figure 5)

Move up one vertebrae at a time from
the sacral or tailbone (4-5 bones)
to the lumbar or waist bones (5 bones)
to the thoracic or chest bones (12 bones)
to the cervical or neck bones (7 bones).

When each vertebra has been moved individual-
ly, rock the entire spine forward and backward in a
long, gentle, wavelike motion, two or three times.
Then move down the vertebrae one at a time from the
cervical to the thoracic to the lumbar vertebrae return-
ing to the coccyx.

Continue moving up and down the backbone until
comfortable. Males practice an odd number of times
(1, 3, 9 etc.); females an even number (2, 4, 6 etc.)

Important Points

The object is to use your consciousness to move
each individual vertebra. The connecting vertebrae
may also move slightly.

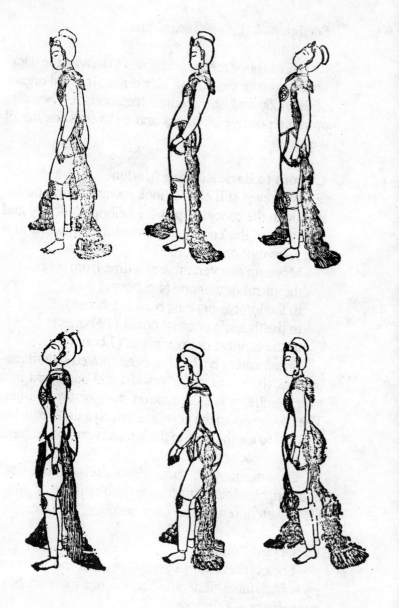

Figure 5

2. Left to Right Swaying Motion

Again begin at the coccyx. This time move the coccyx bone left and right in a gentle swaying motion. Move up the vertebrae in a continuous "S" shape, moving from the sacrum, to the lumbar, to the thoracic to the cervical vertebrae. (Figure 6) Then sway the entire spine forward and backward two or three times before moving down the vertebrae one at a time, ending at the coccyx. Again repeat as many times as is necessary. Males in odd numbers; females in even numbers.

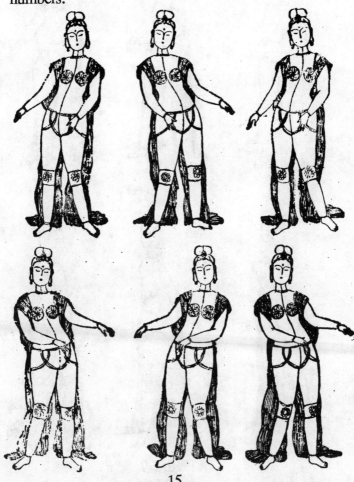

3. Twisting Motion

The third motion is a twisting motion, like wringing a wet towel. Repeat the same procedures for moving up and down the spine as for the former two techniques, except twist each spinal vertebrae. (Figure 7)

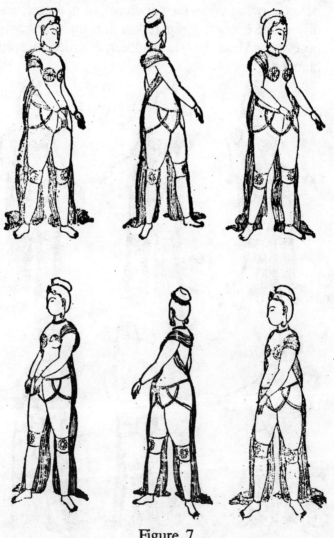

Figure 7
16

4. Combination

Combining the rocking, swaying and twisting motions into one united motion is hard in the beginning and can be a difficult concept to grasp. It may appear to be a rocking motion with a sway and a twist, or it may look like a twisting motion with a rocking and swaying added. Each individual will move in a different way. Only after some practice, will one experience the subtleties of this movement.

Important points

Expanding the third eye and relaxing the perineum are exercises in relaxing the entire body. An old saying says, "One part relaxed, everything relaxed." The following four techniques are techniques of motion. This rocking, swaying, and twisting of the backbone is designed to move the entire body. "One part moved, everything moved."

But relaxation and movement are only techniques. The objective is to develop qi to regulate the body. Excessive attention should not be diverted to the third eye, the perineum or individual vertebrae. Attention should be given to the process as a whole.

Relaxation promotes movement. Movement regulates and changes pent up frustration or overwhelming fatigue. Both relaxation and movement should be practiced with equal attention. Without relaxation or movement, stagnation sets in with no positive results. Relaxation without movement leads to slack and passiveness. Movement without relaxation is like mechanical movement. Sooner or later the parts wear out.

Section 3 Uniting Inside and Outside

This is an extension of the four motion techniques.
As the backbone moves, it causes the internal organs, the joints, muscles, fingers and toes to move. Every part of the body, including the skin and the tiniest hairs, all move and expand with the universe. This is the first step in really freeing oneself.

1. After finishing the combination of movements, with palms facing downward, as the backbone rocks forward and backward, the hands are slowly lifted above the shoulders. (Figure 8)

Figure 8

2. The hands spread apart to the left and right. As the backbone twists left and right, the arms follow, both hands pointing in the same direction. (Figure 9)

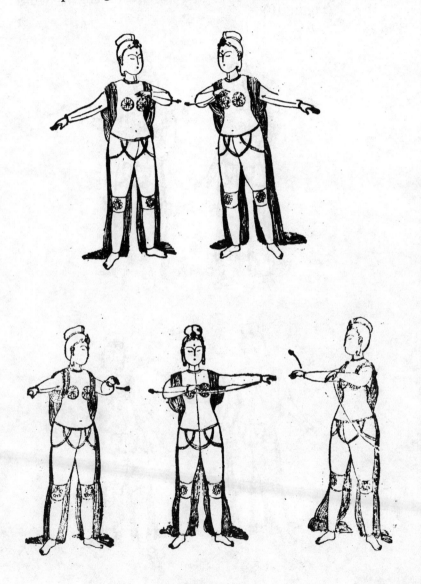

Figure 9

19

3. The hands are held on the left and right side of the body. As the body sways back and forth, the hands come down slowly, like a bird folding its wings. (Figure 10)

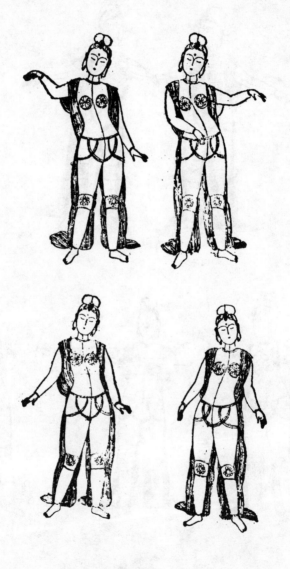

Figure 10

After the arms are brought down, they draw small circles (males 1, 3, or 9 times, females, 2, 4, or 6 times). As the circles are drawn, look inward at the moving backbone. (Figure 11)

Figure 11

21

Section 4   Collecting Qi or Washing the Spinal Cord

This is the last step of the basic techniques.

Bring the arms over the head, palms together. Draw the palms down in front of the face and bring to the abdominal area. (Figure 12)

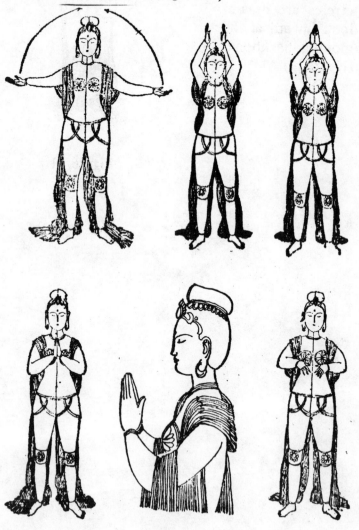

Figure 12

22

Interlace the fingers to form a hand seal. (For males, left fore finger on top, for females right on top.) Place the seal over the abdomen about two inches below the naval. Remain relaxed. (Figure 13)

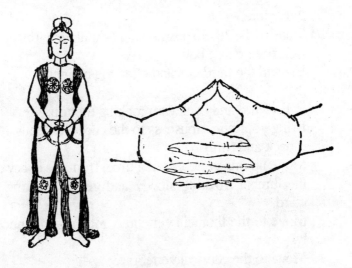

Figure 13

Use your consciousness to move the qi down along the spinal cord and collect it in the abdomen. This is known as "washing the spinal cord" or "collecting qi".

The ancients often said, "If your spinal cord is clean, you can see and perceive." This hints that the spirit is stored in the spinal cord.

After collecting the qi, gently open your eyes.

Section 5
Step by Step Practice for Basic Techniques

1. Clear the mind and prepare for practice.

2. Posture.
Stand in the 70-30 position, feet shoulder width apart.
Relax the entire body.
Expand the third eye and relax the perineum.

3. Forward and backward rocking motion.
Bring your consciousness to the coccyx. Gently rock
it back and forth.
Move up one vertebrae at a time, from the coccyx to
the lumbar, rocking slowly and gently, looking in-
ward.
Move to the thoracic vertebrae, rocking continuous-
ly.
Move to the cervical vertebrae.
Rock the entire backbone, keeping the body relaxed.
Looking inward, "wash the spinal column."
Bring the consciousness down, rocking from one ver-
tebrae to the next. Move from the cervical vertebrae
to the thoracic. Continue rocking down to the lumbar
vertebrae. End with the coccyx.
(May be repeated.)

4. Left to right swaying motion.
Bring your consciousness to the coccyx. Gently sway
it left to right.
Move up one vertebrae at a time, from the coccyx to
the lumbar, swaying slowly and gently, looking inward.

Move to the thoracic vertebrae, swaying continuous-
ly.
Move to the cervical vertebrae.
Sway the entire backbone in an S shape, keeping the
body relaxed. Looking inward, "wash the spinal
column."
Bring the consciousness down, swaying from one vertebrae to the next. Move from the cervical vertebrae
to the thoracic. Continue swaying down to the lumbar
vertebrae. End with the coccyx.
(May be repeated.)

5. Twisting left to right
With your consciousness at the coccyx. Gently twist
it left to right.
Move up one vertebrae at a time, from the coccyx to
the lumbar, twisting slowly and gently, looking inward.
Move to the thoracic vertebrae, twisting continuous-
ly.
Move to the cervical vertebrae.
Twist the entire backbone like you are wringing out a
wet towel. Keep the body relaxed. Looking inward,
"wash the spinal column."
Bring the consciousness down, twisting from one vertebrae to the next. Move from the cervical vertebrae
to the thoracic. Continue twisting down to the lumbar
vertebrae. End at the coccyx.
(May be repeated.)

6. Combination
Bring the hands up in front of the body while rocking
the entire backbone backward and forward.

Separate the arms to the left and right side. Meanwhile, twist the entire backbone from left to right.

Bring the arms down, like the wings of a bird. Meanwhile, sway the backbone from left to right.

Now combine the rocking, twisting and swaying into one gentle motion. Move the entire body, including the fingers, toes, wrists, elbows, waist, and hips in this motion.

Keep the body relaxed as the backbone moves.

The outward movement gets smaller and smaller, slower and slower.

Keep the knees relaxed and supple.

"Wash the spinal cord so that you can see and perceive."

As you move, regulate the inner organs and unite the body with the outside universe.

7. Collect qi.

Bring the hands over the head, palms touching. Gentle drop the arms in front of the face.

Make a hand seal and place it over the abdomen.

Look inward, following the spinal column to the abdominal area. "Wash the spinal column" and collect qi in the abdominal area.

Chapter 2

Wisdom   Techniques

The purpose of wisdom techniques is to develop the third eye. By moving qi through the third eye, down to the earth, up to the heavens and to all sides, one develops qi and stores it for future use. (See chapter 5 for a scientific explanation.)

Section 1 Relax, Expand, Emit and Collect

Before starting these exercises, the first six steps of the basics should be practiced.

1. Relax
Relaxation of the perineum is necessary for relaxation of the whole body. A relaxed perineum opens the body's meridians and permits the circulation of qi.

2. Expand
Hold the hands up in front of the body as if

Figure 14

27

you are holding a large ball. (Figure 14)

Keeping the eyes closed, expand at the third eye. Internalize the combination of rocking, swaying and twisting motions. Bring the consciousness inside the body. With eyes closed, watch the movement of the internal muscles, joints, and organs. Listen to the movement of the body.

Important Points

Breathe naturally. Avoid dragging out or shortening the breath to conform with any movement.

First the perineum, palms and sole should feel warm and slightly numb. Then the feeling should spread to the abdomen, chest, back and entire body. There may be gurgling in the stomach, passing of gas or burping. Do not try to stop this. The body is regulating itself.

3. Emit

Emitting from the third eye enables one to experience the inner smile or "nirvana" smile. It helps rejuvenate the spirit. Keeping the eyes closed, from the third eye, look out and imagine objects as far away as you can. Look for mountains, rivers, stars and the moon. Eventually let your self expand into the universe.

Important Points

This type of emitting is an exercise in using the consciousness to regulate and harmonize the body. It also develops the breathing that regulates the flow of qi. It is similar to the Taoist practice of "Developing qi to unite with the spirit; developing the spirit to unite with the void."

When emitting to the universe, the body should feel as if "it exists, yet does not exist"; "it is empty, yet not empty." This is called void. Only after reaching this stage can one attain realization and wisdom.

4. Collect

After emitting, one must collect. Bring your consciousness back inside your body, and the qi will naturally follow. Bring the qi down along the backbone and store it in the abdominal area, about two inches below the naval.

Important Points

Each person will experience different feelings. Occasionally some may feel itchy, hear birds, smell flowers, see stars, lightening, or colored lights. This is normal. Smile and let whatever occur happen naturally. Some practitioners may not experience these phenomenon. Do not try to consciously seek them. Each person is different.

Section 2   Sink to the Earth and Rise to Heaven

This exercise helps one to expand out of the body into the universe.

1. Sinking

After collecting qi in the abdomen, using hands as guides, bring the qi down the backbone, along the inside of the legs and let the qi sink into the ground as far as it will go. See if you can visualize well water deep within the ground. This exercise develops yin, which nourishes the blood. (Figure 15)

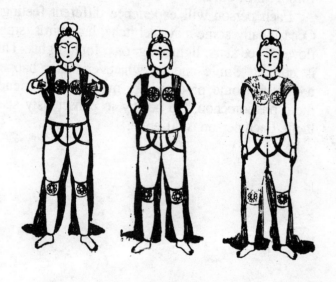

Figure 15

2. Rising

Then using your hands as a guide, bring the consciousness from the depths of the earth, up through the legs. Lifting the hands in front of the body, guide the qi upward, through the top of the head. (Figure 16)

Let the consciousness reach the highest heavens. Imagine the consciousness swimming freely up there. This develops yang, which helps supplement qi.

After a few minutes, bring the consciousness down into the abdominal area.

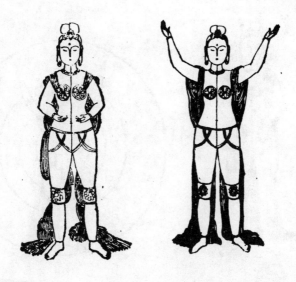

Figure 16

31

Section 3 Expand to All Sides

Let the consciousness expand from the abdominal area to all sides: top, bottom, front, back, left, right. (Figure 17) Emit as far as you can to all corners of the universe.

Feel as if you are breathing with the universe. Let your consciousness stay out of the body for a few minutes.

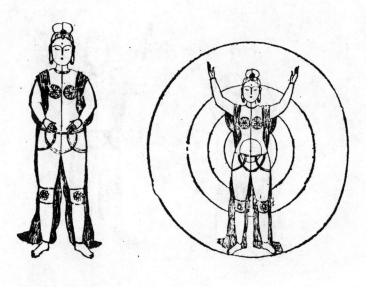

Figure 17

Section 4 Collect the Qi

Bring your consciousness back from afar. Collect the energy from the eight directions and bring it down the backbone into the abdominal area. Listen, look, feel what is in the abdomen. When the consciousness returns to the abdomen, the qi naturally returns. Thoroughly collect the qi in the abdomen so it does not leak. (Figure 18)

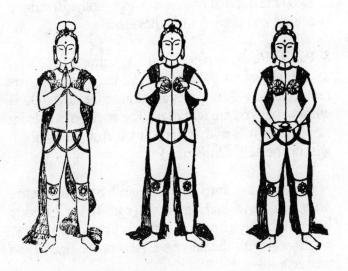

Figure 18

Important Point

The qi that develops in this exercise is good for strengthening the body and preventing illness. It can also develop latent ability.

33

Section 5
Step by Step Guide for Wisdom Techniques

1. Clear the mind. Prepare to practice.

2. Stand in the 30 - 70 position.

3. Practice basic techniques 1 - 6.

4. Keep the internal organs moving gently. Breathing is natural and even. (3 minutes)

5. Part 1 (Relax, expand, emit and collect)
   Beginning with the perineum, the whole body is relaxed. Now exercise your consciousness. Qi is within you; you are within qi. The horizon is in front of you, yet it is within you. Smile from deep down within yourself. (2 minutes)

   Expand the third eye and emit from the entire body. Emit as far and high as you can. The entire body is relaxed. The relaxation expands to infinity -----.
   Breath with the universe. Accept the fate of the universe ------.
   Let your whole body smile with joy. Your joints should be supple. Your entire body should sway slightly. Let your inner body relax, relax, relax. Emit, emit, emit toward the outside. (2 minutes)

   Bring your consciousness back from afar. Store it in your abdomen below your naval. Using your third eye, look inward along your backbone. Collect into your abdominal area.

6. Part 2 (Sink to the Earth and Rise to Heaven)

Beginning with your abdomen, let your consciousness travel along your backbone, down, down, down, into the earth. See how deep the water is. (1 minute)

Let your consciousness rise, up, up, up from the depths of the earth through the perineum, along the backbone. Let it shoot through your crown into the starts. See how high the sky is. (1 minute)

7. Part 3 (Expand in All Directions)

Bring your consciousness down from the sky, back to your abdomen. Emit the qi from your abdomen. Emit, emit, emit to the front, back, top, bottom, left, right, emit from the entire self. Emit to boundlessness; emit to infinity. (2 minutes)

8. Part 4 (Collect the Qi)

Collect, collect, collect into the entire body from the eight directions. Collect into the abdominal area. (2 minutes)

Collect the energy. The consciousness collects the energy from eight directions and keeps it in the abdomen. Listen, look, feel what is in the abdomen. The consciousness returns and the qi naturally returns. Thoroughly collect the qi in the abdomen so it does not leak. (1 minute)

Chapter 3

Combining Yin and Yang

Combining Yin and Yang is the secret of Chan Mi Gong. The goal is to connect man with heaven and earth and eventually unite with the universe.

Section 1 Internal Circles

Before starting this set, it is especially important to regulate the body, the breath and the mind. If the body is properly regulated, then the breath is even and the mind is calm.

The object of the internal circles is to use the conscious mind to lead the qi in circles inside the abdomen. This develops pre-natal or in-born qi.

1. Flat Circles

Place hands over the abdomen about two inches below the naval, males, right over left, females, left over right. (Figure 19)

Using the consciousness, move the qi from the

Figure 19

36

center of the abdomen in progressively larger circles, rotating toward the back and around toward the front. Spiral the circles out toward the waist. Males rotate 36 times, females rotate 24 times. (Figure 20a)

The backbone may twist gently to help move the qi.

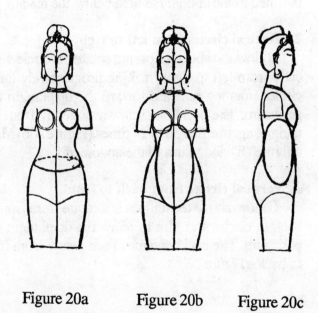

Figure 20a   Figure 20b   Figure 20c

Then make an "S" shape within the circle and reverse directions. The purpose of this yin-yang symbol is to differentiate heaven and earth. (Figure 21)

Figure 21

Continue drawing circles, progressively smaller, 36 times for males, 24 for females, until the qi has returned to the abdominal area below the naval.

2. Vertical circles from left to right

Follow the above steps, but rotate the circle vertically from left to right, making progressively larger circles, rotating outward toward the diaphragm and perineum. The backbone may sway gently from left to right, again either 36 or 24 times.(Figure 20b) Make a figure "S" and return to the abdomen.

3. Vertical circles from back to front.

Follow above techniques but rotate from front to back in circles that aim to reach the diaphragm and perineum. The backbone may rock gently from front to back. (Figure 20c)

Important points

When drawing the circles, do not let the qi spill outside of the skin. Keep it within the abdominal cavity.

The numbers 24 and 36 are used because they have been shown to be effective. After one is familiar with these exercises, the number of circles can be adjusted according to each individual's preference. Males usually rotate in multiples of 3 (3, 6, 9 . . . 36); females in multiples of 2 (2, 4, 6, ...24). However, the number of circles must be the same for forward and backward rotation. This keeps the body in balance.

The internal circles regulate the liver, spleen and kidney. They help in digestion. In general they harmonize the internal organs, especially the endocrine system.

Section 2   Gather Yin from the Earth and Yang from Heaven

The purpose is to develop post-natal qi from heaven and earth. Qi from the earth nourishes the blood and helps develop internal qi.

1. Gather Yin

Using the hands as a guide, palms facing inward, move the qi down along the yin (inner or front) side of the body, from the abdominal area, through the perineum, along the inside of the legs, through the soles, down into the depths of the earth. (Figure 22)

While the consciouses is down in the earth try to visualize clear water and fish swimming. Keep the backbone moving gently.

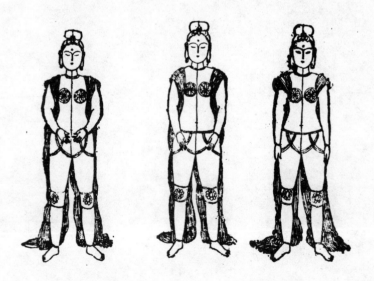

Figure 2 2

40

2. Gather Yang

Still using the hands as a guide, bring the qi up along the yang (outer or back) side of the body, from the heels to the back of the waist to the abdomen.

Continue leading the qi up the back as far as possible. Then part the hands and bring them to the front of the body. Continue to raise the hands, leading the qi up through the head. Shoot the consciousness up into the sky.(Figure 23)

While the consciousness is in the heavens, observe the sun, moon and stars in motion. Keep the backbone moving gently.

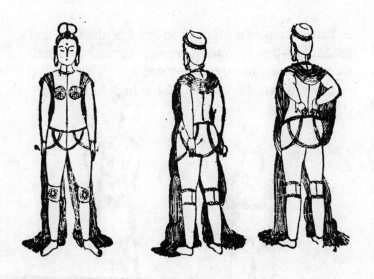

Figure 23

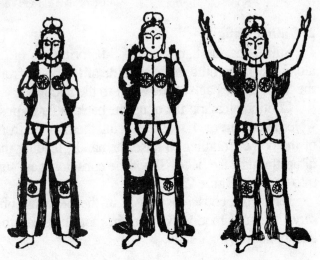

3. Bring the palms together in front of the face and guide the qi down from the heavens, through the head, face and chest into the abdominal area. Then let the qi move down the outside of the legs to the earth. (Figure 24)

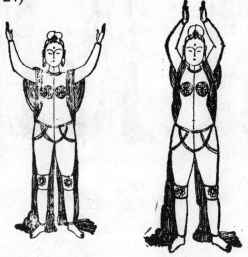

Figure 24

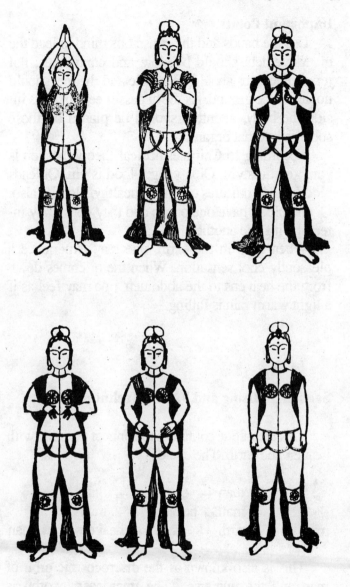

Figure 24

Important Points

Use the hands and the conscious mind to lead the qi. Movement should be slow and continuous, not jerky. The arms should be supple and the feet should not leave the ground. As the qi passes certain parts inside the body, attention should be placed on those specific internal organs.

According to Chinese medical theory, heaven is yang; earth is yin. Qi is yang; blood is yin. Qi leads blood; blood nurtures qi. If qi is healthy, blood is also. Qi and blood have one origin and they constantly interact with one another.

When qi is in the earth, one may experience a pleasantly cool sensation. When the qi comes down from the heavens to the abdomen, one may feel as if a light warm rain is falling.

Section 3 Rising and Falling Techniques

This technique continues to connect the body with heaven and earth. The cycle is

$$man \longrightarrow earth \longrightarrow man$$
$$man \longrightarrow heaven \longrightarrow man$$
$$man \longrightarrow earth \longrightarrow man \longrightarrow heaven \longrightarrow man$$

This is also known as the macrocosmic orbit of man and the universe. (The microcosmic orbit is within the body itself.)

1. Left Side

Using the left hand as guide, bring the qi from the earth up through the left leg. The consciousness, qi and left hand all rise together along the left side of the body until they reach the heavens. Meanwhile the right hand follows along at the side.

The right hand then guides the consciousness and qi from the heavens down the ride side of the body until they reach the earth. The left hand follows along at the side. (Figure 25)

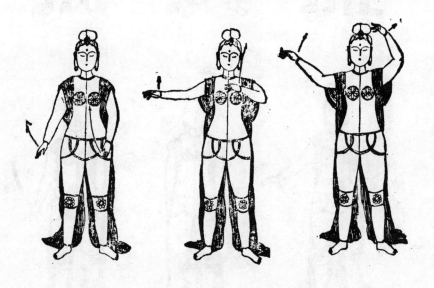

Figure 25

45

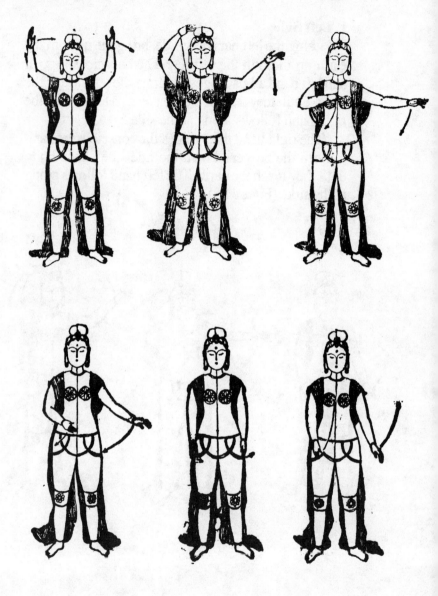

Figure 25

2. Right Side

With the right hand still guiding, bring the consciousness and qi up from the earth along the right side of the body up to the heavens. The left hand then leads the consciousness and qi down from heaven, down along the left side of the body to the earth. (Figure 26)

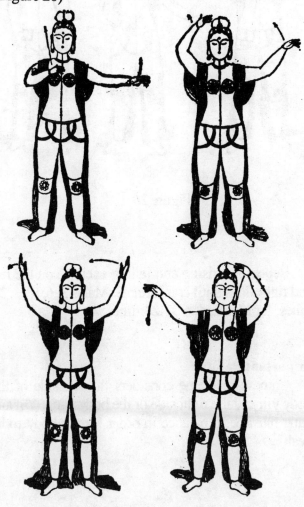

Figure 26

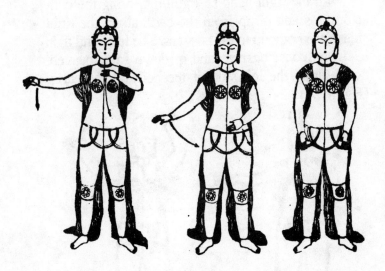

Figure 26

Repeat this rising and falling exercise on the left and right sides until comfortable. Males 3, 6, 9 . . . 36 times; females 2, 4, 6 . . .24 times.

Important Points
Chinese medicine considers the left side of the body yin and the right side of the body yang. Yin and yang must be in balance in order for the body to be healthy.

Section 4 Combining Yin and Yang

This is the final technique of this exercise which combines yin and yang.

1. Using the hands, guide the qi from the earth along the heels, to the outside of the legs, to the waist, to the back, through the head, up to the heavens. (Figure 27)

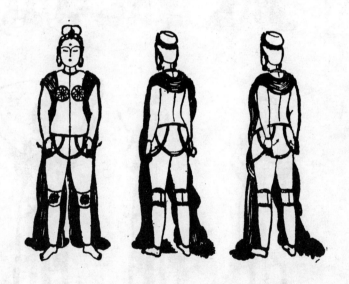

Figure 27

49

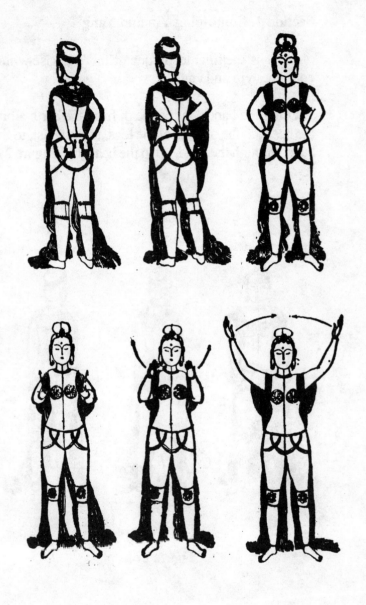

Figure 27

With palms facing, bring the consciousness and qi down in front of the face and to the abdomen. (Figure 28) Collect the qi.

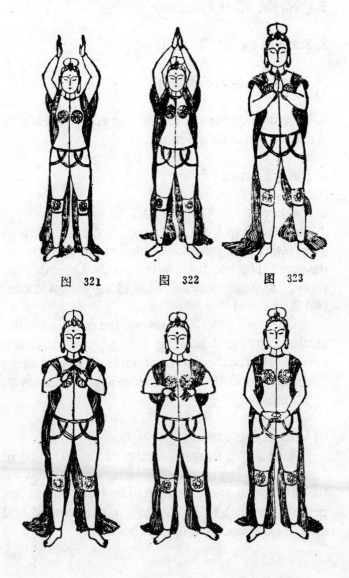

图 321   图 322   图 323

Figure 28

Section 5
Step by Step Guide for Combining Yin and Yang

1. Clear the mind. Prepare to practice.

2. Stand in the 30 - 70 position.

3. Practice basic techniques 1 - 6.

4. Keep the internal organs moving gently. Breathing is natural and even. (3 minutes)

5. Part 1 Internal Circles

a) Flat circle.

Move the qi from the center of the abdomen in progressively larger circles, rotating outward toward the waist. The backbone twists gently. Draw circles, round and steady. Look inward along the backbone. (4 1/2 minutes)

Now make an "S" and reverse the direction of the circle. Continue drawing circles, progressively smaller. The backbone is twisting. Look inward along the backbone. Collect at the abdomen below the naval. (1 1/2 minutes)

b) Vertical circle from left to right.

Move the qi from the center of the abdomen in progressively larger circles, rotating outward toward the diaphragm and perineum. The backbone sways gently from left to right. Draw circles, round and steady. Look inward along the backbone.

52

Now make an "S" and reverse the direction of the circle. Continue drawing circles, progressively smaller. The backbone is swaying. Look inward along the backbone. Collect at the abdomen below the naval. (4 minutes)

c) Vertical circle from back to front.

Move the qi from the center of the abdomen in progressively larger circles, rotating from front to back in circles that aim to reach the diaphragm and perineum. The backbone rocks gently from front to back. Draw circles, round and steady. Look inward along the backbone.

Now make an "S" and reverse the direction of the circle. Continue drawing circles, progressively smaller. The backbone is rocking gently. Look inward along the backbone. Collect at the abdomen below the naval. (4 minutes)

6. Part 2   Gather Yin from the Earth and Yang from Heaven

a) Gather Yin

Using the hands as a guide, move the qi from the abdominal area, through the perineum, along the inside of the legs, down, down, down to the depths of the earth. Down in the earth, the water is clear. Observe the fish swimming. Keep the backbone moving gently. (3 minutes)

b) Gather Yang

Still using the hands as a guide, bring the qi up from the heels to the back of the waist to the abdomen.

53

Continue leading the qi up the back, through the head. Shoot up, up, up into the sky. Observe the sun, moon and stars in motion. Keep the backbone moving gently.

c) Return to Earth
Bring the palms together in front of the face and guide the qi down from the heavens, through the head, face and chest into the abdominal area. Then let the qi move down the outside of the legs to the earth. (4 minutes)

7. Part 3   Rising and Falling Techniques

a) Left Side
Using the left hand as guide, bring the qi from the earth up through the left leg. The consciousness, qi and left hand all rise together along the left side of the body until they reach the heavens.

The right hand then guides the consciousness and qi from the heavens down the ride side of the body until they reach the earth.

b) Right Side
With the right hand still guiding, bring the consciousness and qi up from the earth along the right side of the body up to the heavens.

The left hand then leads the consciousness and qi down from heaven, down along the left side of the body to the earth.
(8 minutes)

8. Part 4   Combining Yin and Yang

Using the hands, guide the qi from the earth along the heels, to the outside of the legs, to the waist, to the back, through the head, up to the heavens.

With palms facing, bring the consciousness and qi down in front of the face and to the abdomen.

9. Collect the Qi

Using the hand seal collect the qi below the naval. Examine the inside of the abdomen as you collect the qi. Gently open the eyes.

Part II

Studies
on
Chan Mi Gong

Chapter 4

History of Chan Mi Gong

Section 1   Chan Sect
by Huang Qian Hua (abridged)

Chan is one of the major sects of Chinese Buddhism. Its emphasis lies on inner contemplation. Thus it is also known as the meditative school.

Bodhidharma is considered the founder of Chinese Chan Buddhism. In the 520's, Bodhidharma travelled from India to Guang Zhou, China. He accepted an invitation from the Chinese emperor and visited him. Later, Bodhidharma went to Loyang and entered the Shaolin Monastery on Mount Song. He sat meditating in front of a wall without speaking, legend says for nine years.

He passed his knowledge on to Hui Ke in the *Lankavatara Sutra*. Then the Chan patriarchate was passed to Seng Can (? -606), Tao Xin (580-651) and Hong Ren (602 -675). After Hong Ren Chan split into northern and southern schools. Shen Xiu (606 -706) is considered the leader of the northern school of Chan Buddhism. Hui Neng (638 - 713) is considered the leader of the southern school.

Hui Neng was a wood cutter who heard people reciting the *Diamond Sutra*. He traveled a great distance to learn more from Hong Ren. Although illiterate, he was accepted as a disciple.

59

Legend says that when Hong Ren wanted to select his successor, he asked the candidates to write a poem, demonstrating his knowledge of Buddhism. The head disciple Shen Xiu wrote on the wall:

Our body may be compared to the Bodhi tree,
While our mind is a mirror bright;
Constantly keep it clean,
And let no dust collect on it.

After reading this poem, Hui Neng had someone write for him:

Originally the bodhi was not a tree,
Nor was the mind a mirror bright;
Since there was not a thing at first,
Where could the dust collect.

Hong Ren recognized Hui Neng's superior understanding, and secretly handed over his robe, the symbol of the role of patriarch. Hui Neng emphasized complete and instantaneous enlightenment. His teachings are collected in *Sutra of the Sixth Patriarch.*

By the end of the Tang Dynasty (9th century), the southern school of Chan Buddhism was further divided into five different schools. In general, Chan schools emphasize direct enlightenment. They stress that everyone possess an inborn Buddha nature that can be uncovered. Each school differs slightly in the exact procedure for attaining enlightenment.

Section 2 Tantric Sect
by Gao Guan Ru (abridged)

Tantric Buddhism or Tantric yoga is considered esoteric Buddhism. It emphasizes reciting of mantras and the use of mudras and mandalas in order to gain inner strength.

Tantric Buddhism first appeared in China in AD 230 with a Chinese translation of the Indian *Matanga Sutra*, which contained many mantras. Mantras are syllables or formulas which hold no literal meaning, but can generate power through repetition of the sounds. Although many mantras appeared in China, they were not especially popular.

Tantricism established itself in China for a brief period in the eighth century. The Indian masters Subhakarashima, Vajrabodhi and others had mastered the secrets of body, speech and mind. They brought in mudras or secrets contained in finger postures and mandalas or diagrams of the deities. They were able to predict rain and cure ill people. Subhakavashima translated into Chinese the *Mahavairocana Sutra*, the basic text on Tantric Buddhism.

But because Tantric thought was so different from other forms of Buddhism, many texts were banned and the meaning in others were changed. Tantric Buddhism did not remain long in the mainland of China.

However, in 840, the Japanese monk Kong Hai learned some Tantric yoga in China. When he returned to Japan he spread this system.

In Tibet, Tantric thought was also more readily absorbed and more firmly established. In the seventh century the Tibetan king Srong-tsan Sgam-po spread

61

Tantric mantras. When Lian Hua came to Lhasa from India, he established the Sang Ye Temple for the propagation of Tantric Buddhism. This is now known as Lamaism.

Section 3 Chan Mi Gong

The exact history of Chan Mi Gong is unclear. Tantric practice have always been shrouded in secrecy and passed orally from master to disciple. Chan Buddhism emphasized sudden enlightenment and paid little attention to written documentation.

What is certain is that Liu Han Wen learned these techniques at home. His great-grandfather, grandfather, father and aunt studied under various teachers and this knowledge was passed on to him. Liu Han Wen systematized these techniques into six sets of exercises now called Chan Mi Gong.

Chapter 5

Wisdom Techniques
and
the Body's Electric Field

The wisdom techniques of Chan Mi Gong have been shown to develop a type of energy similar to the newly discovered electric field of the body.

Chan Mi Gong can prevent illness, strengthen the body, prolong life and develop certain abilities. The results of these exercises have been proven by thousands of years of experience, even though there was no equipment to accurately measure results.

Here lies a fundamental difference in eastern and western scientific thought and philosophy. Eastern philosophy is developed from feeling and sensing to realization of patterns and theories. This is especially true for qigong and Chinese medicine. Chinese herbology has developed through repeated trying and testing. Chinese medicine is based on looking, listening, asking, feeling and finally realization.

Western science is based on precise measurement and the exact function of individual parts. Eastern science is based on the philosophy of balance and overall harmony. Eastern science has its own methods of observation and sets of theories. This is also a science. But it helps to use the measurement techniques of western science to clarify certain points.

63

The physicist Fritjof Capra in his book, *The Tao of Physics,* states "In Chinese philosophy, the field idea is not only implicit in the notion of the Tao as being empty and formless, and yet producing all forms, but it is also expressed explicitly in the concept of qi." The father of the atomic bomb, Oppenheimer, the founder of quantum physics, Heisenberg, and Albert Einstein have all compared principles of physics with eastern philosophy.

Modern science has shown that there is a field around the body. In 1911, Walter Kilner stated that the body has three layers. The first is about 0.635 cm from the body and is dark. The second layer is about 5.08 cm from the body and is lighter. The last layer is about 15.24 cm from the body and is very faint. (Figure 29)

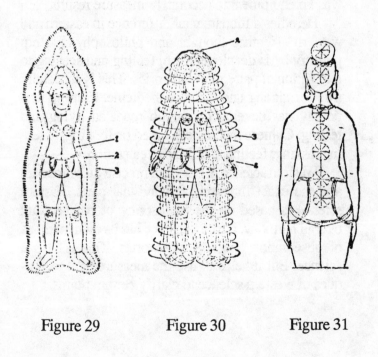

Figure 29   Figure 30   Figure 31

Chakra	Frequency	Endocrine Gland	Part of Body Affected
Crown	972	pituitary	lower brain, left eye, ears, nose, nervous system
Brow	96	pineal	upper brain, right eye
Throat	16	thyroid	respiratory system, vocal cords, esophagus
Heart	12	thymus	heart, circulatory system
Solar Plexus	10	pancreas	stomach, liver, gall bladder
Reproductive	6	reproductive	reproduction
Root	4	adrenal	backbone, kidneys

Chart 1

Further research has shown that a type of electricity moves up and down the spine, and creates a basket like field around the body. (Figure 30). This field contains something similar to electromagnetic waves, but it is not electricity. It consists of nameless particles.

Within the backbone are seven spinning circles of energy sometimes called "chakras." (Figure 31) They correspond to Chinese acupuncture points and western endocrine glands. In a healthy person, these circles are bright, and they spin with a certain vibration. If a person is ill, the circles are dark and they are unstable.

Applying the chakra theory to the wisdom techniques of Chan Mi Gong, we see that the continual movement of the backbone keeps the chakras open and healthy. This in turn has a positive effect on the various parts of the body. (See chart 1)

Exercising this weak electric field of the body, not only can keep a person healthy, it can also be used by mammals to transmit *xinxi*, and it can absorb energy from the universe.

This is only a preliminary study. With the further advance of western science, the mysteries of qigong can be further unraveled.

Chapter 6

Anatomy of the Spinal Column
by Ju Shi Jie

Qigong is one of China's ancient treasures. It can promote health and longevity. Chan Mi Gong is one type of qigong, which is easy to learn, easy to practice and has visible results. Chan Mi Gong exercises the entire body, but emphasizes movement of the spine.

Therefore, some knowledge of the spine will help in understanding the "four movements" and the "70 - 30" distribution of weight.

I. Structure

The anatomical structure of the spine and surrounding tissues is important in understanding Chan Mi Gong.

A. Layers of the Skin

1. Epidermis - The outer layer of the skin consists of pores and hairs. Its function is not crucial in Chan Mi Gong.

2. Dermis - The layer below the epidermis houses hair follicles and capillaries. Movement of this area helps in the circulation of blood and strengthening of the nervous system.

3. Subcutaneous layer - This layer houses sweat glands, arteries, veins and fatty tissue.

B. Muscles

Muscles lying under the skin on the back side of the body help move the spine and adjoining skeletal bones.

1. The outer layer of muscles on the back consist of the trapezes, which is responsible for movement of the neck, and the latissimus dorsi, which helps move the shoulder and arm.

2. The second layer consists of:
a) The levator scapulae and rhomboideus muscles which are attached to the cervical vertebrae and move the shoulder and head.
b) The external oblique attached to the back of the ribs which aids in breathing.

3. The iliocostal muscles being at the back of the hip bone and are attached to the lumbar or thoracic vertebra and a portion of the back of the ribs. They stretch across the backbone and their function is to extend the vertebral column.

4. These muscles are located beneath the iliocostal muscles.
a) Longissiums muscles are attached to the transverse processes of the vertebrae and are responsible for the twisting motion of the spine.
b) The capitis muscles aid in movement of the head.
c) Spinalis muscles are located between the transverse processes of the spine. They help in the movement of the backbone.

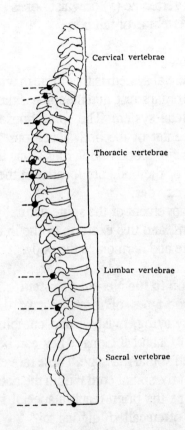

Cervical vertebrae

Thoracic vertebrae

Lumbar vertebrae

Sacral vertebrae

Figure 32

C. Spine

The spine consists of four sections. (Figure 32)
1. Cervical vertebrae (7) or neck bones
2. Thoracic vertebrae (12) or chest bones
3. Lumbar vertebrae (5) or waist bones
4. Sacral vertebrae or tail bone

II. Function

The skeletal system is the frame in which all other tissues and organs rest, and the spine is the central axis of the skeletal system. The spine houses the spinal cord, the center of the body's nervous system. The aorta, the major blood vessel, runs along the spine. All the organs of the body are located in the thoracic or abdominal cavities.

Thus movement of the spine naturally moves the other organs, and this exercise of the internal organs can regulate and harmonize the body.

III. Relation to the Nervous System

The four types of movement of the backbone (rocking, swaying, twisting and combination) form the basis of Chan Mi Gong. They can be considered a type of self spinal massage. These movements of the spine affect the spinal cord within the backbone. This in turn helps the brain reach a special state of consciousness often called "qigong tai."

While in this state of consciousness, concentration on a certain part of the body which is not healthy can help cure the ailment.

This gentle movement of the spine also exercises the internal organs, which in turn regulates the bodies metabolism and prevents illness. It also invigorates

70

the nervous system, which can develop xinxi. This in turn can develop mental ability.

IV. Relationship to Circulation

While practicing the basics of Chan Mi Gong, emphasis is placed on movement of the spine. But this indirectly increases circulation of blood. Blood is responsible for nourishing the cells in the body by transporting nutrients and oxygen. An increase in circulation has a measurable effect on the tissues and organs of the body.

V. 70 - 30 Distribution of Weight

In the natural standing position, a person has a certain distribution of weight. But the 70 -30 position (70% of the weight on the heels, 30% on the soles) redistributes the weight and promotes relaxation of the muscles and joints. It also directs energy up through the spinal cord to the brain. This leads to increased awareness and the ability to balance the body and adapt to the environment.

This position also reduces the tension in the muscles and allows for better flow of blood. The exact function is still under research.

This brief anatomical discussion is a starting point in helping clear up some of the mystery surrounding this type of qigong.

Suggested further reading

Bio-electricity by E. E. Suckling, McGraw Hill Book Company, 1961.

Buddhism in China by Kenneth Ch'en, Princeton University Press, 1964.

The Chakras by C. W. Leadbeater, Theosophical Publishing House, 1927.

Diagnostic Possibilities of Kirlian Photography by Brian Snellgrove, London, 1979.

The Human Aura by Walter J. Kilner, University Books, New York, 1965. (originally The Human Atmosphere, London, 1911)

Human Energy Systems by Jack Schwartz, Dutton, New York , 1980.

The Tao of Physics by Fritjof Capra, Bantam, 1975.